The Job Search Ninja

A Guide to Finding Hidden Jobs Online

Todd Bavol

The Job Search Ninja

A Guide to Finding Hidden Jobs Online

ISBN: 1-4392-3605-4

Cover and Interior Design by Nathan Brown,
Writers of the Round Table Inc.

INTRODUCTION

How many stealth moves do you have? In order to win the best jobs – and ultimately your dream job – in today's world, you have to work like a ninja. Of course, we're not suggesting tactics that are unethical, but your job search must be different than everyone else's. You have to search where others don't search. You must have a strategic plan of attack. And above all, you must utilize all the hidden gems for job searching that the Internet and World Wide Web provide us today. Do you know where to start? Do you have a plan? In this book, we're going to turn you into one of us – a Job Search Ninja - hunting down those coveted dream jobs in places that you'd never expect to find them. By the time you finish and put your plan into action, you will have an arsenal full of stealth moves to land that dream job.

THE EVOLUTION OF RECRUITMENT

Searching for your dream job can either be a daunting task or an adventure depending on how you approach your search. Utilizing new job search tools and having a sense of energy and excitement, should make your job search successful. However, if you approach your search with dread and a bit of gloom, well, similar results will probably follow. In this book, you will learn how to master the art of the job search – online. Utilizing the latest technological resources, you'll quickly find your dream career right around the corner.

To understand job searching today, we must first look at the past. Employment opportunities have always been pretty basic: Our professional culture has developed based on supply and demand. From the industrial revolution to corporate development to the dot com boom, various job categories have developed with the times. So have our search methods to obtain those jobs.

The power of networking still exists today. The motto "It's who you know" still holds true in many job searches. It can be frustrating to find out that the coveted promotion you've been fighting for goes to that other guy – the one who went to college with your boss.

In the past, networking was one of the most common ways people would get jobs, regardless of their qualifications. But it didn't take long for employers to realize that who you know doesn't necessarily translate into what you know, so many companies started paying attention to current staff and recruiting qualified candidates.

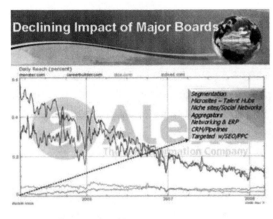

When this happened, reaching out to potential workers through public bulletin boards – yes, the one with note cards and colored tacks – became the norm.

These bulletin boards were very successful in increasing job awareness and even paved the way for classified print advertisements in newspapers. However, when the World Wide Web came along, it didn't take long for companies to realize the value in online job advertising and recruitment. The Internet saved the use of paper, cost less and actually offered employers a larger applicant pool to choose from.

Enter electronic billboards, which quickly became one of the top outlets for employers to recruit new talent. For a job seeker, mastering the use of these job boards was critical. But as more and more job boards became saturated with junk jobs or clogged with too many users, companies moved away from using them and went back to relying on the "who you know" approach.

By now you're probably familiar with job sites like Monster, Career Builder and Dice. Once the "go-to" sites for job searching online, these companies have seen a dip in popularity over the past three years because potential employees were unable to make good matches with employers. It's like being part of an online dating service. If you use it long enough but don't find a good match, chances are you'll look for other ways to create that match.

A MIX OF OLD AND NEW RECRUITMENT TACTICS

Just because these job boards have seen a decline does not mean that they are a thing of the past. The innovative aspect of job searching online is a critical part of the job search mix. If you haven't been online to search for that dream job, now is the time to start. Mastering the various ways to do so is critical to your search success. You just have to know which sites you can use to your advantage and which ones are junk. You have to be your own SPAM filter.

While head hunters still seek out top candidates for many employers, these days companies are looking for ways to save within their HR budgets and act as job vendors to prospective job seekers. Your dream job will not fall in your lap. Your phone isn't going to ring nor will your computer tell you, "You have new mail" if you aren't proactive in your search.

A Survey conducted by Hordes highlights the success rate and current usage of different sources from this type of recruitment. It also signifies a fair warning to those hoping a recruitment officer will simply show up at their door.

Sources of Job Advertisement	% of Job Seekers Benefited	Current Usage % of Job Seekers
Online Sources (net)	30%	94%
Job Board	17%	81%
Online Ad (not job board)	6%	48%
Corporate Career Site	5%	48%
Resume at Corporate Site	3%	50%
e-Newsletter	1%	14%
Blog	-	6%
Friends/ Family Members	17%	55%
Agencies	15%	48%
Employee Referral	13%	46%
Newspaper	12%	49%
School Career Center	6%	23%
Walk-In	6%	17%
Recommendation From Co-Worker	5%	40%

Source – Hordes Survey, 2008

GROWTH PREDICTIONS

Media growth expectations vs. growth in the past five years.

	Five-year annual growth	
	2002-2007	2008-2012
Cable/satellite TV	10.4%	7.3%
Entertainment media	2.6%	5.2%
Newspapers	0.3%	-2.4%
Broadcast TV	2.8%	3.8%
Pure play Internet/mobile	12.6%	14.3%
Broadcast/satellite radio	2.3%	1.9%

Source: Veronis Suhler Stevenson

JOIN THE ONLINE REVOLUTION

Through the Hordes survey and media growth predictions of Veronis Suhler Stevenson, it's clear that the current trend and necessity is to transition from a traditional approach to a dynamic, electronic social approach to finding that dream job.

The facts are there. It's become obvious that in order to remain competitive, a job seeker needs to utilize a proactive, knowledge based approach to identify and seize the best job opportunity.

Using the Power of Technology

WEB 2.0

Chances are, you are reading this book because you know utilizing the Internet's technology is key to finding the ultimate dream job. But where do you start? There are hundreds, if not thousands, of websites that cater to job seekers. Each company incorporates different tools to promote their core values, and yes, their job openings. To "jump online" can be daunting to say the least. So let's break it down a bit. The Web is not just about layers and layers of untranslatable information, funny videos, or a way to avoid paying for a stamp at the post office.

In the world of Internet technology, the term Web 2.0 may sound like the next brilliant edition of software. And in a way it is. If you take the time to understand and incorporate Web 2.0 into your job-seeking thought process, you'll maximize your time and your efforts right from the start.

Imagine reading a favorite novel. You turn each page with anticipation to see where the story will lead you. Well, imagine that in that novel, the characters came alive – literally. What if you could actually ask Romeo how he really felt about Juliet? Imagine asking Tom Sawyer what it felt like to journey down the Mississippi on a raft. Even though we know this can't happen with a novel, in a way it can with Web 2.0. The approach is simple. Web 2.0 makes using the Web interactive. You no longer just read a story on CNN or search for information about a new car you want to buy. Now you can post comments that respond to a journalist's story, and compare features and pricing for that new car. You can chat in your pajamas, shop in your slippers, and yes, participate in a job interview (at least at the beginning stages of the interview process!) without taking a shower. Web 2.0 has transformed the web from a medium to an interactive platform where we can network, share and redefine information through an endless loop of communication channels. Web 2.0 takes existing technology and makes it social.

Here's the difference between Pre- and Post-Web 2.0.

Pre-Web 2.0	Post-Web 2.0
Content focused on theme and design	Information nodes connect to each other with content from users
Website publishers are responsible for the design, composition and organization of the content	Information is syndicated from relevant sources
Information is organized through site map and navigation structure	Information presentation is rendered in conversational format to promote interaction
Users have to read the content	Usage of content maximized through various media presentations
Software downloads are provided in the form of books, utility software, etc.	Portfolio presentation to view the content online in the required format
It is a technology-based system	It is a social environment supported by technology

WHY WEB 2.0 IS IMPORTANT TO YOU

There is no question that the Internet has evolved. And as a result, it has forced companies and organizations to evolve with it. Not even 10 years ago, companies and businesses could afford to choose whether or not to use the Internet to do business. Today, they can't afford *not* to. Nor can you. As more and more businesses integrate Web 2.0 into their company's communications and business way of life, you must understand how that impacts you and your job search. As you search for that dream job, note the companies who utilize Web 2.0 to the fullest. Those are the companies whose business objectives will survive and thrive in the long run.

Further information on web 2.0:
oreillynet.com/pub/a/oreilly/tim/news/2005/09/30/what-is-web-20.html
www.andybudd.com/presentations/dcontruct05

COMMON WEB 2.0 TECHNOLOGY TYPES

To incorporate Web 2.0 to the fullest, you must understand how each piece of interactive technology works.

Podcasts

Podcasts are like recorded audio broadcasts only their files are housed on a website and available for easy downloading. Instead of listening to the latest Top 40 hit while walking on the treadmill, listeners (or users of the podcast) can now learn Spanish or listen to a seminar at a conference they couldn't attend. Because Podcasts are usually in MP3 format, they are easy to download right into an MP3 player, computer or an iPod, making them very portable.

Photo Management

As 35mm cameras become more rare, both businesses and professional and amateur photographers are looking for easy ways to store digital photography – and share it at the same time with others virtually. By housing photography in one place on the Web, managers of this photography can store and organize important work by category and use, plus offer access to it either publicly or through a secure password sign-in system.

Blogs

If you ever wanted a soap box, a blog can be the next best thing. Blogs offer a way for companies, leaders and individuals to express their opinions about a particular topic. But more and more, blogs are being used to interact with the end user, posing questions and inviting the end user to join in on the "conversation." Blogs also allow companies and forward-thinkers to position themselves as leaders and resources for information. Blog styles vary from the casual mom who updates daily on her child's progress at school to marketing and business gurus who lead industries and even our country. End users follow and interact with blogs that have subjects of interest and also receive them through RSS (Really Simple Syndication). Blogs are delivered right to a person's email inbox and offer links for the readers to learn more if they choose.

Satellite Maps

Some may say there is no Big Brother, but those who use online satellite maps like Google Earth might convince you otherwise. Web-based technology now can provide a virtual experience of the world through visual representation and interactive input of geographical elements. You won't actually see cars moving on the interstate, but you can find your own house.

Video

YouTube has become the leader in online video and offers the most comprehensive website to watch and share videos worldwide. There is no question that many videos are fun to watch, but videos are being used more and more as educational tools and to promote company messages and branding. Videos offer an engaging visual experience not just limited to entertainment.

Wikis

Wiki, which in Hawaiian means "Fast," is a software program that allows users to create and manage web pages and build communities on the Internet. The software allows users to create, update and link pages throughout these communities and to share information. Websites linked to similar websites create a collaborative experience for the end user.

ePortfolios

ePortfolios are simply online resumes that are interactive. Instead of having a two-page document that outlines a career path, ePortfolios allow professionals to share personal reflections and achievements with interactive references and links to support the information.

This tool allows for professional updates, providing a way to demonstrate new achievements and open newer areas of social and professional recognition.

Social Bookmarks

Similar to the basic bookmarks of favorite sites stored in a personal computer system, social bookmarks are collected to share with others. Users add social bookmarks to a website to share the content with other users interested in the topic.

Online Groups

Web communities gather those who share similar interests together. These user groups share related information through the use of web tools.

Social Networks

Social networks were introduced by Web 2.0 for individuals and organizations to establish contact. These social sites fuel online networking by forming relationships with like-contacts and are excellent for building professional relationships. MySpace, Facebook, LinkedIn, and Twitter are just a few of the popular sites being used today.

Voice Thread

Voice Thread is a collaboration tool to combine multimedia with text, Voice Thread supports audio, video and text to help users communicate. It is an ideal tool for audio conferences and group conversations.

Scrapbooks

Much like paper scrapbooks, digital scrapbooks use the concept of gathering pictures and ideas to tell a story, but with the added benefit of multimedia support. These can be downloaded or printed as per user requirement.

Virtual Worlds

Virtual worlds are literally online worlds composed of visual content that allows users to interact with other users in an online environment.

SUMMARY

There is no question that Web 2.0 has opened the door for remarkable online interaction that used to be considered "cutting-edge" and is now an integral part of daily life online. For job seekers, it opens an amazing door of opportunities:

- Creating professional contacts worldwide through social networking

- Sharing an ePortfolio of professional accomplishments with the push of a button

- Efficiently launching a resume to various recruiters, hiring companies and field professionals

WEB 2.0 ASSESSMENT #1

What type of company do you want to work for? Think about your core values and then make a list of five companies that share those values. Then visit each company's website and subscribe to their blogs. After you've read their blogs for about a week, create a list for each company that details what was important to them during that week. Did you learn anything new about these companies that you might not have known if you'd just read their home pages? How will this new information affect the way you think about these companies? Do you still want to work for them?

2.
Internet Search Engines

The Internet is a vast and powerful machine. How do you break through the clutter to find exactly what you are looking for? Search engines (Google, Yahoo!, etc.) allow you to find exactly what you want – or at least pretty close to it.

Search engines are actually built to *avoid* spam. Any website with spam is identified and penalized by the search engines. Some companies have found a way around this, but for the most part, sites are built and designed to optimally work within the search engine world to give you what you need.

It works like this:

Search engines produce results based on a query you enter. For instance, you want to search for a job in the entertainment industry. In the Google search field, you type in "jobs in Hollywood." From that query you might then see a results list of thousands of websites to choose from. You can then narrow your search by being more specific and eliminate those sites that have no relevance to the information you need.

Search engines work on three main concepts. They are:

- Spiders or Bots

- Indexing function

- Ranking of websites

Further information on search engines: en.wikipedia.org/wiki/Search_engine - computer.howstuffworks.com/search-engine.htm - searchenginewatch.com/2168031

SEARCH ENGINE PROCESS

There are different search engines available online that work through automatic processes, manual entries and partially manual versions. Some websites are even embedes search engines. This is done using commercial software, and makes it simple for guests to remain on the site while still gathering information unrelated to the hosting site.

Search engines have their jobs cut out for them. Of the thousands, if not millions, of websites in existence today, it is the search engines' job to rank and file these websites according to relevance and usage. The higher the ranking, the more credible the website probably is for your use. Website designers and marketers create identifiable tags and keywords that search engines look for. The better "indexed" the designer is with these keywords, the more relevant the results will be when you search.

Because designers are adding new sites to the Internet daily (if not hourly), using directory listings for each site doesn't necessarily authenticate the quality of the site. Authenticating every new site is virtually impossible. Therefore, using a directory can be useful in locating niche information or websites that have lost their significance for general search usage.

HOW DO SEARCH ENGINES INDEX AND RANK WEBSITES?

Crawlers are automatic processes run by the search engines to ensure that fresh pages and content are included in the search results. Crawlers or spiders scan the Web and index the reachable pages by visiting them. The more often content is updated on the website, the higher the ranking. This denotes that the website is very "active."

Spiders looks for active links, extract them and then index them for review. Spiders crawl through web pages on a scheduled timeframe to index any changes to the website. Some users and hosts avoid spiders because if the web design includes forms, frames or image maps, spiders do not read this format, ultimately preventing web pages from being indexed.

UNDERSTANDING THE TERMINOLOGY BEHIND A SEARCH

Stop word lists are words with no meaningful contribution to the words being searched. Examples are "an", "the", "a".

Word stemming technique is used to create base words from the words given by stripping the suffix. For example "jobs" become "job", "searching" becomes "search". This can be termed as canonization of words to extract the relevant keyword.

Thesaurus is used for creating a search that identifies synonyms for the words given by the user. Capitalization is ignored during search.

Page design and content plays a major role in search engine results. Frequency of words occurring in the different areas of a page plays a significant role in indexing. It is always better to have optimized usage of keywords in the content. This is called search engine optimization or SEO.

The next factor is *theme links*. How do pages interact with each other? Which pages link to what within the website? Search engines review websites that have intuitive links and then rank them accordingly.

Meta tags are used by search engines to help in easy identification of the website theme and content. Word construction is vital, as "job search" creates a better match solution than "search for a job". For experienced web users, knowledge of meta tags can optimize search engine use.

For *inbound links* originating from different websites, relevant keywords have an impact on search engine results. Other factors include design considerations, HTML conformity, frequency of user visit and paid sites.

Note: Many users know search engines sell site placement - where a site will appear based on search results - so placement often identifies a site as paid or advertised to visitors.

Live page: Live web pages are pages with frequent content updates and changes. Search engines require a website to be active in order to be included within their search results. This helps avoid outdated pages popping up within a search. The more active a site, the higher the ranking in a search.

SEARCH USING SEARCH ENGINES

What really happens when you type in "job search?" There is a methodical series of steps that search engines use to fetch the most relevant links and websites.

1. What you type in the search engine is then processed through a query analyzer.

2. A query analyzer functions as a clause identifier to extract the clauses for search.

3. Clauses are words linked by words such as: and, or, either, neither etc.

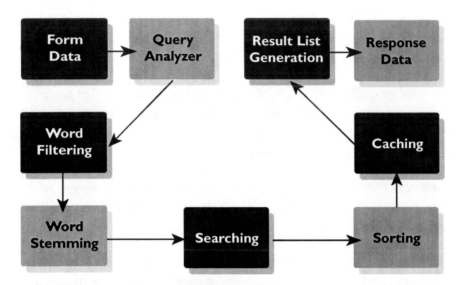

Everything is filtered using stop words lists. So the process includes filtering out words like "an", "the" and "a". The query clause is then constructed with the relevant words, allowing for search results to be sorted and cached. Caching keeps track of the information stored across many pages, so if you want to refine your search for more specific results you can.

The sub query extracts those websites that should be the focal point from the search results, and your search is complete.

POWER OF BOOLEAN LANGUAGE

French, German, Spanish – all websites must speak one common language in order to be recognized by search engines – and that's Boolean.

When you were a kid, your parents probably said things to you like, "It's a little cold to be playing outside." Those types of comments were vague and you simply knew you couldn't go outside. As you got older, you came to understand the underlying meaning, or subtext, of what your parents meant – they wanted you to play indoors – but when you were younger you didn't understand the complexities of the language. You only understood exactly what your parents told you.

The Internet operates the same way. It only understands exactly what you tell it – and you have to tell it in the right way.

Search engines return results based on the search query entered. If you enter information that a search engine doesn't understand, it won't respond the way you want it to.

Search terms play an important role in search results. Search results can be improved by inclusion of synonyms, common terms, and possible spelling of the term. In order to get the best results from your search, you must constantly tweak your search terms to fully utilize the search tools and language within the search engine. This will get you the best results.

WEB 2.0 ASSESSMENT #2

How are you going to use search engines to your advantage? Make a list of all the keywords or adjectives and words that describe the type of job you are searching for. Create broad, sweeping statements like "environmental jobs." Then create more specific searches like "environmental jobs Massachusetts." Take a look at the different results for each. Which one provided you more with specific links to jobs that you truly were looking for? Continue to refine your words to determine which ones will produce the best results for you.

3

The Power of Right Search

USING GOOGLE SEARCH

One might argue that Google is world-dominant when it comes to search engines. So, if you're going to start searching for your dream job, Google is the best place to begin.

Smartly enough, Google's domain name is www.google.com.

Enter the search keywords you want to use and click on Google Search to find what you're looking for.

Search terms used in Google are automatically constructed using 'AND.' For example, if the search term is Jobs Houston, the search engine queries for results for Jobs AND Houston.

FINDING FOCUSED RESULTS

If, on the other hand, a user simply wants to know about jobs in Houston, the use of quotation marks will eliminate the AND plus construct phrases. Quotation marks help in searching words occurring together and provides more focused results. For example, use "Jobs" + "Houston".

FINDING SYNONYMS

Another option is using the tilde ~ sign in front of a word. This allows the user to search for a word as well as its synonyms. For example, if you want to find all relevant information for the word "career," type in ~career and you'll receive information that includes the words "career", "job" and "employment". This gives you a way to create a broader search.

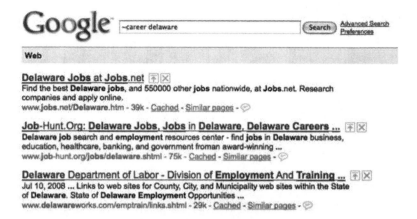

Sometimes general words used in search queries can result in false positives. Take a look at your results. If they aren't specifically what you're looking for, try the same search again but add a hyphen (-) and then the word you want to eliminate from the search. In the search for Job Resources, the results are dominated by Human Resources. So the search term is tweaked to Job Resources –Human

SENSITIVE TYPING

Take care of how you actually type in your words and symbols when creating a search. Google reads each character in a certain way. In the example above, you'll see there is a space before the hyphen to distinguish between the minus operation and hyphen words. Minus usage must always be preceded by a space before the minus (hyphen) sign. When you include hyphen, apostrophe, and equal to symbols, search engines will treat the words as phrases.

You can use the plus sign in the same way as minus to add to your search. A search term Job +consultancy yields results with job consultancy occurrences while the search term Job consultancy yields results with other forms of consultancy such as consultant. Don't forget the correct spacing when you use the plus sign as well.

Another option is to use the word OR. This allows inclusion of an alternate word to guide the results. Remember that words bound by OR are mutually exclusive. The word OR must be in capital letters. Job OR opportunity generates results with either job or opportunity in the content.

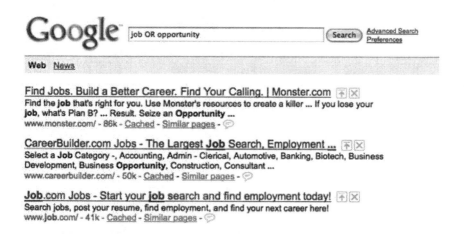

Asterisks (*) can be used as wild cards to replace any word. It is most useful in search terms where a particular word in the middle varies and the other two words remain constant.

So, obviously creating the best keywords for a search is not necessarily just about the words; it's how you string them all together. In addition to the common symbols noted above, here's a "cheat sheet" of other terms that have specific meaning and function in Google searches. Be sure to use these terms followed by a colon (:).

Usage	Result	Example
Define:	Definitions and abbreviations from the net for the word	Define: job
Weather:	Returns the weather condition	Weather: New York
Time:	Local time around the world	Time: New York
Stocks:	Returns the stock prices	Stocks: msft
Phonebook:	Returns the address details and acts as a phone directory for residential phones	Phonebook: Thomas

USE GOOGLE TO DEVELOP A TARGET LIST

So, now the goal is to use Google to your job search advantage. Instead of crawling through human resources websites like Monster and Yahoo! HotJobs, you can now create specified, targeted searches with Google that will produce results not just on these jobs sites but many others, as well as company sites. If a company posts a job opening in multiple locations, your Google search will find them. Utilize the tools above to create targeted searches that produce optimum results.

GOOGLE ADVANCED SEARCH OPTION

Instead of "hand-creating" targeted lists with contact names and addresses to companies that you'd like to apply to, you can now use Google to create these lists for you. For example, a focused search on accounting companies in Delaware can provide specific contacts to reach out to in a job search. You can do this through the advanced search feature on Google.

Google advance search also provides you with a way to search with OR conditions, and exact phrases.

The placements of the text with respect to the conditions are illustrated below.

Plus, file types such as PDF, DOC, etc. can be specified, or specifications can be made to search only certain domains.

ADVANCE FUNCTIONALITIES IN GOOGLE

Google searches can be as simple or advanced as you make them. It all depends on keywords, conjunction words and the advanced features of punctuation or query modifiers.

PUNCTUATION

Originally, Google replaced punctuation automatically, but it now accepts underscores and ampersands. For you, it means that companies or businesses with ampersands in the name will be picked up in a search, whereas before they wouldn't and that could have been your dream job!

QUERY MODIFIERS

Some commands have specific functionality to them and, when used, should be followed by a colon (:).

1. **intitle:** This command searches for the first search term in the title and the rest of the terms in the content. For example - intitle: Accounting Audit will return search pages with accounting in the title and audit in the content.

2. **allintitle:** This command searches for the occurrence of all the search terms specified in the title. For example - allintitle: Accounting manager returns search pages with accounting manager in the title.

3. **inurl:** This command searches for first search term presence in the URL. For example - inurl: accounts will return search results where the url has accounts mentioned.

4. **allinurl:** This command will search for the presence of all the terms in the URL. For example - allinurl: accounts manager jobs returns all the URLs with accounts manager jobs mentioned.

5. **allintext:** This ensures that pages have the specified search term and do not return any links embedded in the pages without the search term. For example- allintext: accounts controller will find some pages with no search term visible. This only qualifies and ensures the return of pages with the words "accounts controller" in it.

6. **allinanchor:** This command applies a search to embedded links from the main pages. It is not mandatory for the main pages to have the search terms. Allinanchor and allintext perform exactly the opposite. For example -

<u>allinanchor:accounting</u> will produce a search where all the links with the keyword "accounting" are included in its page.

POWER OF QUERY MODIFIERS

Don't underestimate the power of query modifiers. They take a bit of getting used to, but once you determine which ones will work well for you, they have the ability to create extremely targeted searches. Take a look at the following example. This search was conducted for audit controller jobs without a query modifier but with the allintext query modifier.

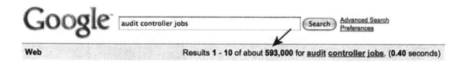

A normal search for audit controller jobs returns a result of 593,000 results, while a search with query modifier allintext results in 276,000 results. While your results produce much fewer hits, the hits that it does produce offer a much more targeted and focused result.

TIPS TO IMPROVE RESULTS

Getting too many results? Improve the focus by ...

- Introducing a phrase or a word
- Searching the results from a domain or site if feasible
- Fine-tuning the search term
- Removing generalized words if possible
- Preventing obsolete sites from the search results by including date

WEB 2.0 ASSESSMENT #3

You just read a lot of information about how to tailor a Google search that meets your needs and criteria. Chances are, you didn't remember half of it on the first read-through but that's okay! Many times these features will stick with you better if you actually do them. So here is a worksheet to put your newfound knowledge to work. Keep this last section of the eBook handy, and refer back to it as often as you need to. Before you know it, your searching technique will become second nature!

I. Search and compare the number of results for the following exact phrases.

Phrases	Search Hits
Consultant jobs	
Functional consultant jobs	
Functional consultant finance jobs	

2. Search for the Finance or Accounting jobs in Delaware.

Advanced Search Options	Values		
All these words			
This exact wording or phrase			
One or more of these words			

Refine the search term to search for finance jobs in Delaware.
Repeat the search to find the number of hits for accounting jobs in Delaware.

Search Purpose	Search Term	Search Hits
Finance jobs in Delaware		
Accounting jobs in Delaware		
Finance or Accounting jobs in Delaware		

3. Sites may represent jobs as employment, career, opportunity, vacancy. Search for any synonymous terms that represent job.

The search has to be executed for Delaware finance jobs.

Search term used in the search window	
Number of hits	

Search to be done: Delaware finance with alternate forms of "job".

Search term used in the search window	
Number of hits	

4. The most important aspect of a job search is finding fresh job openings. Execute a search for Delaware finance or accounting jobs posted within one week. Compare the earlier executed Delaware finance or accounting jobs hits.

Choose to use Google search or Google advanced search as appropriate.

Search	Number of hits
Delaware finance or accounting jobs	
Delaware finance or accounting jobs with Date range	

5. It is common to find part-time, temporary and contract jobs while searching for accounting jobs in Delaware. Search for ONLY full-time accounting jobs in Delaware. It can be executed including this specification in the search term or by negating part-time, temp and contract.

Search for Delaware accounting jobs with full-time.

Search	Number of hits

Delaware accounting jobs without part-time temp and contract

Search	Number of hits

6. The name of the company with suitable openings is identified. Most organizations store the job vacancies in an ATS system, which search engines typically don't index. If you're looking for a job at a specific company, you visit the career page on their company's website for more information.

a. Company name is Johnson & Johnson Inc. Search for the URL of the company.

Search term	URL of the company

b. Use the URL to obtain the employment / career / recruitment website of Johnson & Johnson Inc.

Search term	URL of the recruitment company

c. Visit the website and try for different results. Think of other ways of gathering information from the site using Google Search and the power of query modifiers and search tools. Remember that technology continues to evolve and Google continues to enhance its search features. Check back often to find out what new tools have been invented to give you an even more targeted search.

4.
Job Sites vs. Job Search Engines

As you continue to break down your options for advanced job searches, you'll want to turn to the specifics of job search engines. Job sites like Monster.com, Careerbuilder.com and Yahoo's Hotjobs are sites where employers post available jobs, whereas job search engines allow you to create advanced searches to collectively find jobs posted on both job sites and company sites. Examples of these types of sites include Indeed.com, SimplyHired.com and Jobster.com. They do the searching for you and dive into multiple locations looking for your specific criteria.

Although specific job sites offer access to a wide selection of positions available, they are limited to only what an employer actually posts to the site. Time is money, so to speak. It's more time-effective to use the websites that combine results found on all job search engines instead.

JOB SEARCH ENGINES

Job search engines excel in efficiency. In just one search, job seekers can collectively find all of the target jobs on the big three job sites in just one search. Believe it or not, job search engines are actually even more powerful than Google.

Job search engines have the ability to hone in and focus on the specific jobs you're looking for and provide tools to make your search even easier. Using keywords like the type of employer, date of job posting, location, and type of job are easier to search for through job search engines.

For example, search for a finance job by typing "finance" in the keyword. A list full of variety appears, including jobs for a finance controller, finance manager, finance executive, and finance consultant. You don't have to creatively think of different ways to search for "finance;" the search engine does it for you.

Job search engines are also current, a feature that is extremely important in a competitive job search market. They receive instant information through syndicated feeds, whereas traditional search engines add fresh content only on a scheduled "cycling" basis. You'll definitely have a competitive edge using job search engines.

To that end, job search engines offer email alert sign up. Once you have created a profile of the type of job you're looking for, the job search engine remembers your dream job (or jobs) and searches for them automatically. When it finds one, it zaps you an email. You can then immediately apply for the job, showing a potential future employer that you're on your game. Take heed, however. Job search engines pull from multiple sites, sometimes retrieving duplicate listings of the same job. You may be excited about seeing your dream job more than once, but don't apply more than once. You'll shoot yourself in the foot with that future employer before you even grab an interview!

Take a look at how the three most popular job search engines perform against each other.

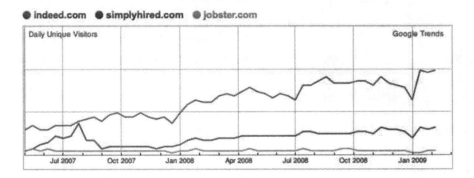

Remember that accounting job in Delaware? We decided to create a search for that job with Indeed.com, SimplyHired.com and Jobster.com. Take a look at how focused the results are.

www.indeed.com

accounting jobs in Delaware   Jobs 1 to 10 of 498

Indeed.com returned 498 hits.

www.simplyhired.com

Simplyhired.com returned 568 entries with the same search criteria.

www.Jobster.com

Jobster.com identified 373 entries.

HOW THE BIG THREE JOB SEARCH ENGINES STACK UP

INDEED.COM

Walter Mossberg of the Wall Street Journal correctly hailed this site as "simply a one-stop shop for job seekers." For those savvy at Google searching, Indeed. com's advanced search engine is a breeze to use. There are also plug-ins available to help navigate your search in even more detail.

Plug-ins are found on the Tools page. These specialty programs allow you to adapt the job search engine functions to whatever web browser you might be using and to sync the website with the browser to maximize search functionality.

Make sure you're always notified immediately of new job opportunities by signing up for the Job Alerts either by email or IM, too.

SIMPLYHIRED.COM

As of February, 2009, SimplyHired.com's database included five million jobs worldwide and has now entered into content sharing partnerships with heavy hitters like CNNMoney.com.

Its goal? To become the largest online database for job searches all while streamlining the entire search process to make it more efficient and save time for users. Whether you're looking for a position in a traditional career or something that might be part-time or a position in the wilderness, SimplyHired.com searches for those unique type of jobs as well.

SimplyHired.com allows users to come full circle with social networking as well, which today is on the rise as far as business networking and finding new opportunities. Through SimplyHired.com you'll be able to create synergies with Facebook and MySpace, add widgets for search engines like Google, and receive cell phone alerts, too.

If the job you're looking for is a Fortune 500, non-profit or Forbes listed company, SimplyHired.com provides special filters that refine your search. Seeking part-time or stay-at-home positions? Job seekers will find part-time search options, as well as a search for working mothers and family friendly companies.

Finally, Simplyhired.com offers tools to evaluate a particular industry over a certain period of time. This affords you the opportunity to take an educated guess on whether or not your chosen career will be around for the long haul.

JOBSTER.COM

Jobster.com differs from Indeed.com and SimplyHired.com in its functionality.

Indeed.com and SimplyHired.com are job search engines while Jobster.com is a network of career-based sites. It integrates all aspects of Web 2.0 including people, jobs and opportunities to ultimately improver your overall career. You can even go back to school at Jobster University and take classes that will give you an edge over other employees in your field of expertise.

GETTHEJOB.COM

GetTheJob.com incorporates patented technology to build job portals for organizations to advertise their available positions currently listed on their own ATS systems. Job seekers can use Google with appropriate keywords and search terms in order to find these jobs.

JOBMAPS.US

Perhaps your dream job is not really a dream "position" but a dream "location." Looking for bookkeeping positions in Hawaii? Want to teach English as a second language in Miami? JobMaps.us allows job seekers to find jobs based on location. Using maps, JobMaps.com visually assists with looking at unique traits of a job like the proximity to downtown, train stations or airports.

For those searching for a position outside of a familiar area, understanding a job location before applying can save hours in the search process. Too many times, applicants waste time papering companies they would never work for because of the companies' location.

NICHE JOB SITES

A final area to look into is those sites formulated for niche positions. Although many may not feel their job is that unique, exploring these sites may open up hidden career opportunities.

Beyond.com is the largest niche website, focusing on specialized careers in various fields. Other sites, such as LatPro.com, capitalize on the growing bilingual culture within the United States.

A few of the executive career sites worth visiting with a large number of executive and senior executive positions are Notchup.com, Theladders.com,

Careerjournal.com. These sites focus on recruiting executives drawing a salary of $80,000 USD and above. They create a database of executives and provide a platform for companies to identify and recruit candidates. There are also other executive recruitment sites that work on prescreening the job postings to ensure that the jobs posted cater to the executive level. Membership to these sites is more often by invitation and close scrutiny of the application.

Just getting started in your career? Many specialty sites where internships and summer jobs are posted are designed specifically for college grads and entry level professionals. For example, MonsterTrak.com is affiliated with Monster.com and an excellent site to consider.

Work for a union? Consider scouring through industry specific jobs that are posted to your professional organization or union websites. You'll find a complete list of organizations and unions at the American Society of Association Executives' Gateway to Associations.

For everyone else, here are additional niche job site options.

Industry	Website
Information Technology	Dice The IT Job Board ComputerJobs.com
Finance	eFinancialCareers.com Jobsinthemoney
Hospitality	Hcareers.com Caterer.com
Retirement	Retirement Jobs
Security	BrokerHunter.com
Government	GovernmentJobs.com
Bio/Pharmacy	Medzilla.com
Call centers	Callcentercareers.com

Clearance	ClearanceJobs.com
Communications	TalentZoo.com
Construction	MEP at Work
Engineering	Engineering Central
Healthcare	Allnurses.com
Human Resources	Jobs4HR
Insurance	Great Insurance Jobs
Legal	LawJobs.com
Leisure	Leisure Jobs
Linguist	Top Language Jobs
Logistics	JobsInLogistics.com
Marketing	Marketing Jobs
Media	TVJobs.com
Post Military	Destiny Group
Retail	AllRetailJobs.com
Sales	Sales Jobs
Sports	JobsInSports.com
Teaching	eTeach.com
Telecommunications	Telecomcareers.net

WEB 2.0 ASSESSMENT #4

Pick two or three job search sites, create searches and sign up for email alerts. Then monitor each one's results for a week. How many provided you with duplicate job listings? Which ones gave you accurate and potential leads that fit your professional career track? Do you need to eliminate one because it isn't providing the results that you wanted? If so, revisit the list and try a new one. Continue to assess these sites until you find three to six that deliver targeted job leads to your inbox on a weekly basis.

5.
Mastering Social Networking Sites

Remember, about 40 percent of the jobs out there are still landed not because of what you know, but who you know. Social networking can serve as an equally powerful tool to get you the job you want. Personal referral is still one of the top ways to land that dream job, and social networking sites like MySpace, Facebook and LinkedIn are designed to create the "Six Degrees of Kevin Bacon" syndrome. Uncle Joe's brother's friend's sister may be on Facebook, and through social networking that "who you know" thread might help you find your next job. As in any networking, traditional or otherwise, knowing someone who's connected with the job you want or the company you want to work for automatically gives you a leg up on the competition.

WHAT NOT TO DO ON SOCIAL NETWORKING SITES

Remember those three blurry days in Key West? How about that party with your college buddies that involved a pool, some fish and a keg? While it's fun to share these memories with your closest friends, potential employers probably aren't going to want to see this "fun" side of you. So when you post photos to your social networking profile, or any information for that matter, keep it fairly clean and professional. Studies have shown that companies often research a candidate's online behavior along with reviewing professional references and work history when considering someone for a position.

The following chart shows the percentage of behaviors flagged by recruiters when researching a candidate through their online, social networking profile.

Percentage of Flagged Behavior	
Drinking or using drugs	41%
Inappropriate or provocative photos	40%
Poor communication skills	29%
Bad-mouthing former company or employees	28%
Lying about qualifications	27%
Using discriminatory remarks related to race, gender, etc.	22%
Unprofessional screen name	22%
Linkage to criminal behavior	21%

Excerpt from Career Builder.com online survey conducted by Harris Interactive.

This just proves how much your personal life and your professional career truly intertwine in today's technological society.

According to Rosemary Haefner, Vice President of Human Resources at CareerBuilder.com, "Hiring managers are using the Internet to get a more well-rounded view of job candidates in terms of their skills, accomplishments and overall fit within the company."

Here are the precautionary measures Haefner suggests when using social networks:

1. Clean up digital dirt. Make sure to remove pictures, content and links that can send the wrong message to a potential employer before you start your job search.

2. Update your profile regularly. Make sure to include specific accomplishments, inside and outside of work.

3. Monitor comments. Since you can't control what other people say on your site, you may want to use the "block comments" feature.

4. Join groups selectively. While joining a group with a fun or silly name may seem harmless, "Party Monsters R Us" may not give the best impression to a hiring manager. Also be selective about who you accept as "friends."

5. Go private. Consider setting your profile to "private," so only designated friends can view it.

Always take the necessary steps to maintain a professional image on accessible online networking sites. Finding that new job may depend on it.

POPULAR SITES

Now that we've covered the "What happens in Vegas" warning, here is a breakdown of some of the most popular social networking sites you might be interested in exploring.

All of them contain unique factors that will help aid you in creating a social network to further your name recognition, career knowledge and overall job search. There are many sites. Choose just a few (maybe the ones that you know friends and colleagues are on so you can quickly build your networks) and then focus on keeping those few active and current with the latest information about yourself.

FACEBOOK

Celebrating its fifth birthday in February 2009, Facebook claims dominance simply because it seems like everybody is on it. Well, they practically are. Facebook boasts a whopping 150 million members worldwide - more than the population of some countries! This includes the average joe, corporate executives, politicians, moms, celebrities… the list goes on.

Imagine linking with new "friends" around the world. What about that high school sweetheart you haven't heard from in 30 years? Or the amazing college English professor who got you started in writing novels? When you create your original profile, Facebook asks for detailed information such as the high school you went to, college you graduated from, what city you live in, etc. From there, you can actually join groups or networks that already exist that will help you find those long-lost people. On a professional level, this can help you link up with contacts in a city or area faster, keep your finger on the pulse of what's happening in a certain city, or reach out comfortably to someone you met only once at a party.

The saying "Don't talk to strangers" is thrown out the window a bit when you're using social networking sites, and it's not uncommon to reach out to a complete stranger to ask for a job lead. Why is this okay? Because you and the stranger have the ability to "qualify" this contact by saying "so and so" suggested I be in contact with you – and then by simply clicking a button both of you can confirm that it's okay to be connected. And as we mentioned before, many of the social networking sites work in tandem with the job search engines like SimplyHired. com, which offers a plug-in to manage your search efforts on Facebook.

STATUS

What are you looking for? Networking? New friends? A job? Specific organizations? By denoting in the status section of your profile exactly what it is that you want to get out of using Facebook, you let the Facebook community know what's important to you. "Always open to the right opportunity" is an ambitious but ambiguous message to let others know you'll leave your current position if something better comes along, but should keep you out of trouble with your current boss.

INTERESTED IN

Announce your skills. This is an excellent option because if you're trained to analyze x-rays but work as a secretary, why would anyone think to tell you a position at their hospital has become available? Make your special skills known.

EDUCATION

This links up to Facebook's networking system in order to connect you with fellow alumni potentially working in your field. Or other alumni who know someone who does.

EXPERIENCE

Here's where you get to toot your own horn. This section gives you the opportunity to showcase former employers that are registered on Facebook and may connect you with former colleagues, supervisors or bosses that can help you move your career ahead.

GOLD STARS

Be nice to everyone, because gold stars can come from people that know you or have worked with you. Receiving positive feedback can help give that little extra push to someone who may have been considering offering you a referral but wasn't sure whether or not it was the right choice. Gold stars are referrals too – they are testimonials about who you are and what you can accomplish for a potential employer. These are coveted, so treat them with care.

LINKEDIN

From a business and professional perspective, LinkedIn is probably the most popular social networking site. Millions of professional contacts with seemingly endless resources are ready to network and share opportunities. LinkedIn even

includes members from Fortune 500 companies so you clearly will have access to some impressive heavy hitters if you become a member.

The developers have made creating an account very easy, even for the average computer user, and the features are simple to navigate.

RECONNECT

Remember that brilliant co-worker who always had fantastic ideas during brainstorming sessions? "I wonder where he is now?" With ReConnect you can find out. The program is designed to root out where you've worked, lived and studied and connect you with the people from those times.

POWER YOUR CAREER

A handy tool if you are trying to move up the corporate ladder, Power Your

Career can help you find insider information on who is hiring and where – but subtlety. After all, while searching for that dream job, you still need to maintain professionalism with your current employer and don't want to become a part of "water cooler" gossip.

GET ANSWERS

There is no better way to get ahead in the workplace than by being inquisitive and continuing to learn new things about your job or industry. Get Answers enlists experts in various fields, who answer questions you post, offer advice and discuss successes and failures. In a way, these experts become mentors, and can help guide you into the best possible position for your skill set.

TRIBE

Find your community on tribe.

Are you thinking of relocating and looking for a job in a city that you're a bit unfamiliar with? Tribe creates communities of users within specific towns. So if you were thinking of finding a job in Los Angeles or want to brainstorm with current residents there about job opportunities, you might join the Los Angeles tribe to get the inside scoop.

Tribe also includes a section with local job postings or you can reach out to your new "friends" in the tribe to let them know you're looking for a specific job, allowing you to constantly keep your ear to the ground about what's going on in a city of interest.

MYSPACE

MySpace isn't necessarily only for the young these days, as more and more people understand the value of social networking, regardless of the perception of the site.

Although it is great for any age group, MySpace is probably best suited for a younger professional looking to make new contacts, build friendships and foster relationships.

RYZE

Looking to "rise up" through the ranks and climb the corporate ladder? Named for this notion, Ryze is all about networking. There are more than 1,000 different organizations posted on Ryze, with the sole purpose of connecting professionals with like-minded interests.

Most of its services are free, but Ryze also offers paid memberships for advanced searches. The site is home to more than 500,000 members based in 200 countries around the world. While Ryze is geared for all professionals, many of the groups are geared toward women, making it an excellent networking resource for women.

THE CAREERMOLE

CIA agents. Secret service. Planted moles. Yes, they do exist in social networking and you definitely want to befriend them. The difference is, on CareerMole, the "moles" are actually very upfront about who they are and why they are socializing on the site. CareerMole actually markets itself to companies for their recruitment purposes. The mole's main mission: to create a liaison between current team members with a particular employer and with potential company candidates. Employees are recruited by CareerMole to service as ambassadors, offering input and advice to those interested in working for a particular organization.

The open invitation to reach out to someone working in your dream office is a fabulous concept, and that relationship should be developed as carefully as it would if you were meeting them in person. The reason? When jobs are available, the Mole is the one to hit up for an endorsement.

And the best part is the HR department loves it. The Mole is constantly developing relationships for HR and offers endorsements for online candidates they've connected with when a position does become available in the company. If you plan ahead and develop a quality relationship with a Mole at your dream company, your chance of getting an interview for a coveted position increases substantially.

TIPS FOR DEVELOPING A QUALITY RELATIONSHIP WITH A MOLE

- Be professional! The number one rule in professional social networking is to always communicate on a level that is professional. All of your correspondence should be politically correct, positive and career-motivated – at all times.

- Start a conversation. Reach out to the Mole to introduce yourself, clarifying that you are interested in more information about the company the Mole represents.

- Be prepared to follow up. When the Mole responds to your initial hello, follow up promptly with a list of appropriate questions for the Mole regarding his company. Three questions is an appropriate number to get the conversation going. More than that, and you might be quickly labeled a "Chatty Cathy."

- Thank the Mole for his or her time. Suggest setting up a meeting to chat further, either through a quick phone call or at a social event.

- Keep in touch. Reach out to the Mole with career updates or something appropriate to his or her company (i.e. an article you saw, a fact you read) once a month.

- Be alert. The moment a position you are interested in opens, reach out to the Mole and express your interest. As you have developed a relationship with the Mole, the odds of your resume making it to a decision maker are much higher than a cold call submission.

WHAT NOT TO DO WITH A MOLE

- Waste time – yours or the Mole's. Make your emails and meetings concise and professional at all times.

- Gossip. There will always be that Mole who is unhappy with his or her job and will want to vent. Do not get caught up in these conversations. Anyone willing to vent about others will eventually vent about you.

- Lie. It's a small world, and if you lie about yourself or your current career, you're setting yourself up for professional embarrassment and limiting your future opportunity.

- Stalk. Use discretion in reaching out to a Mole. There's a fine line between interest and desperation, and creating a negative impression is just as powerful as creating a positive one.

NETWORKING FOR PROFESSIONALS (NFP)

NFP maximizes all the features Web 2.0 has to offer. From encouraging members to post video footage, photos or portfolios within their profile, Networkingforprofessionals.com helps members make the most of technology while utilizing the personal touch.

NFP carefully monitors their site to ensure members are there for the mission statement of the company - "bringing together successful, motivated professionals." If that's not your reason for being there, don't join.

NFP was developed in New York in 2002 and is quickly expanding across the nation with branches in Arizona, California, Florida, Georgia, and Illinois.

With NFP, location is critical as this combines the philosophy of online networking with live networking events.

NFP HOSTS HANDS-ON EVENTS SUCH AS:

1. Shakers and Stirrers Business Networking Mixer

2. High Speed Networking (yes, networking built on the idea of speed dating!)

3. Power Lunch

The following is an example of local events listed on the NFP site.

TIPS FOR NETWORKING AT ONLINE SPONSORED LIVE EVENTS:

- Prepare your pitch. Be ready to describe, in fifteen seconds or less, what you currently do and where you see yourself going.

- Dress the part. Arrive at a networking event dressed as you would arrive at an interview.

- Paper your contacts. Have professional business cards close at hand, preferably with links to your online networking profile.

- Follow up. When you meet connections at a live networking event based around social marketing, it's critical that you take the time to reconnect online with the contacts that you've made. Social networking sites recommend setting aside 30 minutes a week to maintain contact and further develop online professional relationships.

SUMMARY

The advent of Web 2.0 has provided some outstanding tools for social networking. Thanks to the genius behind those who recognize the importance of fostering relationships to build a career, many of these sites are devoted to creating those connections that can help you advance.

Taking advantage of many of these social networking sites allows you to position yourself as a viable candidate who is current with the latest trends and skills and connected within your industry.

Remember, with social networking, the key factors are:

- Be professional

- Be accessible

- Be consistent

As long as you maintain these traits, you will present an inviting image that says you are going places to the other professionals in your field – and potential future employers.

WEB 2.0 ASSESSMENT #5

If you're not already involved in social networking, it's time to dive in. If you are, good for you – but are you utilizing all the features for your professional career, or is it more casual? Pick two or three social networking sites that fit the genre of people and organizations that you want to be involved with, then create your own profile for each. Each day, spend 30 minutes to an hour, collectively, on these sites, reaching out to new leads, creating new connections and friends. You may want to start with just one site to get a feel for the interaction that goes on, or simply "watch" the action for awhile before you become active. Be sure to integrate social networking into your career search and make it just as high a priority as you would talking face-to-face with friends about the fact that you're looking for a new job.

6.
The Passive Job Seeker
Branding Yourself as the Most Sought After Candidate

Now that you've learned how to actively and effectively promote yourself on the social networking sites, it's time to consider the opposite approach to finding your ideal job opportunity – becoming the passive job seeker.

EXCERPT FROM FEBRUARY 2009 PRESS RELEASE

THE RIGHT THING, INC.

… AIRS, a company of The RightThing and ZoomInfo, the most comprehensive source of business information on people and companies, today announced an expanded partnership and a powerful set of new solutions for recruiting professionals.

Taking integration to the next level, the expanded partnership will provide corporate recruiters and HR professionals using the all-in-one talent solution AIRS SourcePoint, with unrivaled free access to passive candidates through ZoomInfo's database of more than 45 million professionals and 5 million companies.

Existing and new customers of SourcePoint can now seamlessly search via name, company and title for ZoomInfo profiles…

"Integrating ZoomInfo into SourcePoint's robust pool of over 3,000 job boards allows us to continue to deliver unmatched recruitment technology to the market and provides our clients with the most complete solution to meet their growing needs, *"* said Chris Forman, President of AIRS. *"Keeping pace with the challenges of this economic downturn, corporate recruiters can depend on AIRS to push the envelope in delivering powerful tools that enable them to reinvent how they find passive and active candidates."*

THE PASSIVE JOB SEEKER

"I'm not really looking." How many times have you heard that from someone when you ask if he or she is searching for a new job? They may just say that, but in reality, most everyone is usually looking for better opportunities, whether actively or passively. The passive job seeker is a new corporate buzzword heard at the recruitment and HR levels. Defined as someone who is not actively searching for a job, the passive job seeker may not actually be passive at all. However, until proven otherwise, companies are eager to attract those who fall into this category in the latest trend of corporate hiring.

Here's why:

- Already employed, a passive job seeker is an untapped resource – hopefully, an undiscovered diamond.

- A passive job seeker has up-to-date training and contacts within the industry.

- A passive job seeker is (seemingly) content with his current position and therefore, (seemingly) an excellent asset to his or her current company.

Major recruitment companies have partnered together to combine their resources in hunting for passive candidates. ZoomInfo is an online resource used by recruiters and corporations to search for them.

ZOOMINFO'S PRODUCTS

X-RAY SEARCH

What does an X-ray do? It looks beyond the surface and into the core of something. So with this tool, recruiters have sneak peeks at networking or career sites such as LinkedIn without joining the site, and can pull specific information based around

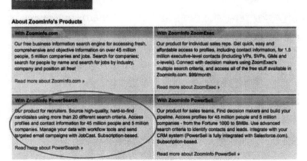

what they need. The technique gives recruiters a snapshot of a particular area of expertise or job location. For instance, a company in Austin, TX wants to see what passive candidates might exist for an engineering position. An X-ray search will show this.

Using Boolean search techniques, a recruiter can also enter the name of the social networking site coupled with the position available and the location but *subtract* the url directory and find the similar information.

Search: *Site:www.linkedin.com engineer Austin —inurl directory*

FLIP SEARCH

Here's why it is so critical to have your resume online, and links to it in your social networking profiles. In flip searching, potential employees are found through live links to their resumes. According to Brian Weis, president at Recruiters Network, the Association for Internet Recruiting, "The use of flip searching or flipping is a technique to mine the Internet for potential candidates."

Weis explains it like this: "For example, John Recruiter is looking for ORACLE Programmers. This technique can be used to find the various sites that are linked to Oracle.com. In theory, John will find people who have online resumes with Oracle skills because they may have linked to Oracle on their online resume."

This technique is so powerful that Weis warns that in rare cases, searching can sometimes connect the searcher with the intranet (internal internet) of an organization. This can provide access to private company email lists and databases which, obviously, are not materials the company would authorize anyone to access. Taking advantage of this find would be illegal, of course, but it does show an apt demonstration of the potential power behind flip search techniques.

BECOMING A PASSIVE CANDIDATE

So how do you become a "proactive" passive candidate? Knowing that companies actively search for passive candidates, positioning yourself as a passive candidate is a smart way to put your resume at the top of the heap.

BUILD AN E-RESUME OR HOMEPAGE

You don't have to be Internet savvy to create an e-resume or homepage that markets who you are. There are many companies out there with templated, professional designs that can do this for you. But before you dive in to having a home on the Web, take some time to review your resume to ensure that what you're posting won't get you passed over, passive or not.

Tips for building an outstanding resume:

- Open with a career summary. Years ago, resumes would start with an objective. Today, an objective flags a potential candidate as inexperienced. Create a brief, five sentence pitch to encapsulate who you and where you intend to go as a professional. That way, if a recruiter only reads the first five sentences of your resume, he or she will know what you are all about.

- Include a Career Highlights section immediately following your summary. Career highlights should be bulleted and focused on metric-based achievements. For example: Transitioned follow-up billing to an electronic format, resulting in $80K fee recovery within the first three months.

- Focus on metrics throughout your resume. Practically every sentence should include a quantifiable, specific example of your achievements. Note: Mind confidentiality within your metrics. Your company may have a policy against you discussing specific numbers, so include percentages instead.

- Format. A professional resume should look professional. If you are not adept at creating formal documents, enlist the assistance of a friend or colleague.

- Proofread. It should go without saying, but poor grammar or incorrect spelling will not prove you are mindful to detail. Triple-check your work or have your resume professionally edited.

Now that you have created a professional resume that reiterates why you are the ideal candidate, it is time to post it on the Web for key passive candidate positioning.

A SEARCH-FRIENDLY RESUME

"Build it and they will come" doesn't necessarily apply here if your online resume isn't optimized and easily searchable. Just like creating specific keywords to search for a job, you now must make sure *your* resume includes keywords that others would use to search for *you*.

As a passive candidate, your resume needs to link up with all the keywords that might crop up first in a Boolean search. Therefore, tracking down these words and phrases, then finding a clever way to weave them into the body of your resume, is critical.

EXAMPLE:

- You may be an account executive. Your resume contains that phrase but...
- Corporate account executive is the more popular term used on job sites.

Somewhere within your resume, include the term. For example, "Experience working with top corporate account executives on high profile accounts" or "Received phi-sigma training for adept communication with corporate account executives."

This is how companies "write" their websites so they are noticed in search engine searches, so why not do the same for your resume? Ultimately, you're just like a consumer company, trying to get your product (that's you!) noticed.

WEB 2.0 ASSESSMENT #6

Research key terms found in positions you would apply for on sites like Indeed. com. Then take a look at the example of the search completed below, for an accountant position in Delaware. Immediately, it's easy to see the descriptive word "high" is popular.

Now that you've pulled up a list of positions available, delve in deeper and review specific postings. Here is the position of a Senior Staff Accountant with select phrases circled.

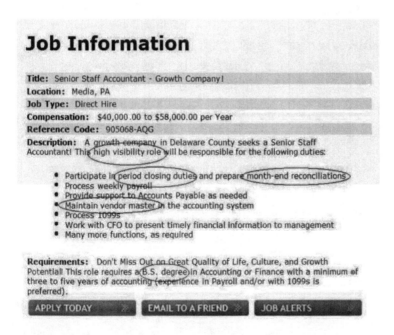

Job Information

Title: Senior Staff Accountant - Growth Company!
Location: Media, PA
Job Type: Direct Hire
Compensation: $40,000.00 to $58,000.00 per Year
Reference Code: 905068-AQG
Description: A growth company in Delaware County seeks a Senior Staff Accountant! This high visibility role will be responsible for the following duties:

- Participate in period closing duties and prepare month-end reconciliations
- Process weekly payroll
- Provide support to Accounts Payable as needed
- Maintain vendor master in the accounting system
- Process 1099s
- Work with CFO to present timely financial information to management
- Many more functions, as required

Requirements: Don't Miss Out on Great Quality of Life, Culture, and Growth Potential! This role requires a B.S. degree in Accounting or Finance with a minimum of three to five years of accounting (experience in Payroll and/or with 1099s is preferred).

APPLY TODAY   EMAIL TO A FRIEND   JOB ALERTS

So how do you really search for what others are searching for? You need to know what others are using for search words and phrases within the sites, and then incorporate those words into your resume.

Try this: Search the job sites for the positions you are interested; in then make note of the key words and phrases that seem to continually pop up in the ads you read. Make note of them on the following charts.

POPULAR PHRASES	POPULAR DESCRIPTIVE TERMS

Review your resume and find where those popular words and phrases could replace your words or phrases, yet still maintain the same meaning of your expertise as it's explained in your resume.

PHRASING TO REPLACE	WORDS TO REPLACE

Once you have replaced your typical terms with more popular search engine terms, the odds of making it through a company search or a recruiter search are much higher.

7.
The E-Resume

Your resume is now you perfect selling tool! However, all the bells and whistles will mean nothing if your resume can't be found online. Creating an E-Resume allows you to post your resume online so it will be found. Here's how:

1. **Create a Blank Format**

    Change the formatting of your resume by going to Save As on your dialog box and saving your resume under Text Only or Plain Text. When you reopen the file, open it using NotePad, WordPad or Simple Text.

2. **Make it Computer Readable**

    Select all and change the font to 12 pt., simple-to-read Arial font. Change anything italicized or bolded into plain, simple font.

3. **Create Headings**

    Put your name, address, email and phone number each on their own line. In between each, leave a blank line.

4. **Use Your Keywords**

    Utilizing your work from above, transpose those keywords into your resume.

5. **Create Hyperlinks**

    Include web-friendly language to link up with various websites. Strategically place links to your company's website, affiliations and organizations you are a part of and clients you have worked with. For example, if you once worked for Yahoo!, include Yahoo's! link, www. yahoo.com next to the dates that show when you worked there.

POSTING YOUR RESUME ONLINE

Remember, you are still working under the premise that you are a passive candidate and aren't necessarily proactively searching for a new job (although secretly you may be). To post your e-Resume online you can either upload your resume to a free site, or build your own professional website and post the resume as part of its content. If you have the time and the resources, building your own web presence is the best choice, because it shows potential employers that you are smart and understand the value of doing business professionally. Here are a few pros and cons to each method:

PROS TO BUILDING A WEBSITE	CONS TO BUILDING A WEBSITE
Professional presentation	Small financial commitment
Opportunity to showcase more than resume	Takes more time to build
Maximize Web 2.0 opportunity	Slightly advanced skills required

PROS TO POSTING JUST AN E RESUME	CONS TO POSTING JUST AN E RESUME
Free	Less professional presentation
Fast	Not as convincing that you're really a passive candidate
Simple	Cannot maximize benefits of Web 2.0

If you're still trying to determine which method is best for you, Microsoft has designed a simple and free step-by-step program through Office Live, also known as B Central. To get started, visit Office Live at www.officelive.com.

HOW TO UPLOAD YOUR E RESUME

At Office Live, you will be able to post your e-Resume on your account and leave it there for recruiters to stumble across.

To get started, a simple sign-in process will require you to enter your name, email address and type of employment.

Before posting your resume, you'll be asked to verify your account through an email verification process. Once that is complete, you can easily post your resume by following the prompts that appear on the site – and simply upload your resume.

Now you are a passive job seeker!

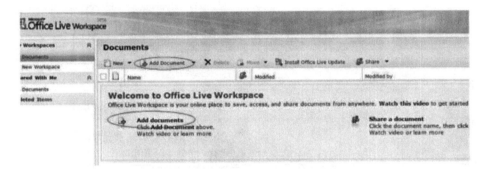

CREATE AND POST A WEB SITE

You don't have to be a full-time web designer to create a simple yet professional website about yourself. Office Live also provides tools and step-by-step instructions on how to create a website that fits your needs.

TIPS FOR BUILDING YOUR SITE

Your website is not a place to post the latest pictures from your five-year-old's gymnastics class. The sole purpose of this site is to market yourself and be recognized as a passive candidate. To that end, it is critical to keep the content of your site 100 percent business. That way, when your clever positioning leads Boolean searchers to your front door, they will be 110 percent impressed with what they see.

The following are tips to make your site more professional, engaging and search engine friendly:

- Make your contact information easily accessible

- Include a link to your company's website

- Include links to clients you have worked with (check into your company's confidentiality agreement before doing this one)

- Include a testimonial page from past co-workers who can attest to your outstanding skill set and professionalism

- Include links to any and all social networking sites you are on

- Include links to any volunteer organizations you are affiliated with

- Post a professional photograph – be certain you've dressed the part or don't post it

Now get started! Visit www.officelive.com to create your account and your website, which will include your e-Resume.

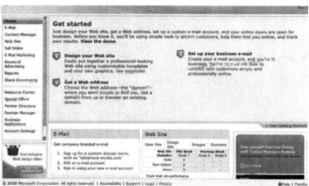

BLOGS

Blogging today can be a dad writing about his first fishing trip with his son, or a corporate executive giving insider tips about a new trend in an industry. What is most important about blogs is that they tell something about you. It could be a personal tidbit or it could showcase your professional knowledge and expertise in a particular field of employment. Of course, we want to focus on the latter here when creating a blog as a passive job seeker. Ultimately you want your words to position you as an expert or knowledgeable professional who any recruiter would want to have. In order to make your blog viable, however, it needs to be active. Creating a blog and then only posting once a month won't have an impact. A blog that includes a new entry every two to four days will get noticed not just by recruiters but by search engines as well. And lastly, make sure the information in your blogs is correct and error-free. Like anything else, you can sink or swim your credibility if you have a blog that makes you look unprofessional or unskilled in your industry.

There are many free blogging sites available today including WordPress and Blogger.com. The latter was purchased by Google in 2002 and is one of the easiest ways to get started with posting a blog online. It uses all of the features of Web 2.0, making it possible to post video and photos as well as blog text. The following screenshot displays some of the features of Blogger.com.

NEWSGROUPS

Just like locals hanging out in the corner coffee shop, recruiters are known to hang out in newsgroups. Join a newsgroup, speak knowledgeably about the topic at hand, and you're sure to be noticed. Use technical language when possible and offer your opinions. A recruiter isn't going to spend time in a newsgroup if all he hears is "chatter" from technical engineers – he can find a million of those folks anywhere. But he will spend time in a newsgroup tracking the conversation of those advanced technical engineers who may have the skills for the position he's seeking to fill. Discussing terms that only someone in your field would understand is the best way to pull focus towards you by a recruiter on a newsgroup board.

Tips for standing out in a newsgroup:

- Speak wisely. Include several terms within your conversation that only someone in your field would understand.

- Get involved. Ask questions of other experts and answer questions posted.

- Offer a resume link. On your sign-off, include the link to your resume or website as part of your professional signature.

ONLINE COMMUNITIES

Online communities are similar to newsgroups, but a little less information-based. Still, taking the time to join up with online communities affiliated with the position you have or, better yet, the position that you want, is a key opportunity for you to continue to create a positive and professional online presence that leads back to your resume.

SUMMARY

If you ever wanted to create a bit of mystery and allure about yourself, then passive job searching is for you. However, you must be proactive to be passive. Yes, it sounds like an oxymoron, but in order to be noticed, you must take the time and the steps to create a resume rich in keywords and then establish an online presence through your e-Resume, blogs, newsgroups and online communities. Recruiters are looking for standouts, not someone who simply appears in the hiring pool and then jumps at any job that comes along. Having your resume handy and accessible with the click of a button helps put your contact information at the fingertips of recruiters and into the hands of the companies you want to join.

WEB 2.0 ASSESSMENT #7

Create an online presence. Decide whether you simply want your resume posted online or if you want to go a bit further and build your own simple website. Who are your trying to attract? If you could choose recruiters from any company, where would they be from? Learn all you can about that company and what their recruiters are looking for and be sure to incorporate them in your e-Resume and other areas of your website. In addition, start blogging two to three days a week either on your own blog or commenting on a blog that belongs to a company you'd like to work for. Start to build your online presence and continue to update it on a weekly basis.

8.
Marketing Yourself

At the end of the day, searching for a job, regardless of your method, is really all about self-promotion. Some people are great at it (especially those already in the fields of marketing and sales) while others might feel a bit uncomfortable about being aggressive and putting themselves out there. Where do you fall in this spectrum? Having an understanding of your comfort level of marketing yourself will help to determine which methods of Internet marketing are best for your own personal pursuit of your dream job.

USING THE POWER OF THE INTERNET FOR SELF-MARKETING

In general marketing terms, branding is synonymous with identity. What is the identity of a certain product? Coca-Cola is known for, "Have a coke and a smile." BMW and Mercedes-Benz conjure up images of luxurious, expensive and elite. What is your identity? How do you want to brand yourself? Once you determine that, the opportunities online to market yourself are simply endless. Therefore, you must create a quality plan of attack for finding your dream job to avoid spreading yourself too thin.

Top Tips for Self-Marketing

1. Maximize your social network

2. Add email marketing campaigns

3. Volunteer

4. Utilize creative techniques

5. Employ direct marketing

Let's think about business and marketing for a minute. Any great marketing or sales plan has a timeline to it. It's carefully thought-out and it is measurable. You know how to implement a program and then measure the results. If it works, fantastic! If it doesn't, you return to the drawing board to re-evaluate what worked and what didn't; and then you refine your plan again. The same holds true for these five key steps in branding yourself online. Create an action plan of your own or check out the calendar tools that Microsoft Office has created that can help you to create a plan and stay on task.

MAXIMIZE ONLINE SOCIAL NETWORKS

If you're not careful, you could find yourself partying till the wee hours of the morning on Facebook. It is important to spend at least a half an hour a week on social networking sites, reviewing profiles and reaching out to professional contacts. The more fruitful contacts and leads you discover the more time you'll need to invest. Take heed, however. These sites can literally suck you in, simply because they're so fun! Stay focused, remember your goals and stay on track.

Tips for Marketing Yourself Using Social Networking Sites

- Update your profile constantly. Many of these sites send out alerts to let your "friends" know that your site has been updated. This is a way to get your name in front of people as often as possible, without it coming from you personally.

- Be a cheerleader. One of the best ways to get noticed is to notice other people and their accomplishments. If someone in your field has recently received a promotion or an award, what a great excuse to get to know them. Offer your congratulations along with your introduction. Just be sincere about it.

- Make a hit list. Troll through those who are already members of your dream companies on sites such as CareerMole. Make a goal of reaching out to five people per day. By the end of the month, you will have potentially added a whopping 150 contacts to your social network.

- Get personal. Once you have established relationships with those on your social networking site, get personal, be brave and bold. Set up meetings over coffee or over the phone to meet new people and garner leads within the industry.

- Attend network gatherings. Spend time researching the different gatherings posted on these sites for professionals in your field. Make a goal of attending at least three networking events per week, armed with your business card. Follow up with all of the live professional contacts you make.

EMAIL MARKETING CAMPAIGNS

How many email newsletters do you receive a week? A day? One of the most powerful marketing tools today, e-newsletters are a professional way to talk about new trends, points of interest or to begin discussions about problem-solving with your contacts. It indirectly markets you as a leader in the industry and a resource for information – clearly something any prospective employer would want in an employee.

Several low-cost services are available online to help you create an email campaign. These services will help you to:

- Compile your email lists to make them comprehensive and manageable

- Create newsletters to update and inform your colleagues of accomplishments, goals and the fact that you are always willing to consider a better position

- Run an email promotion

Tip:

Do not waste time signing up for a free trial. Although many of these trials may be long enough for you to land your dream job, you will lose your carefully compiled email list. Your best bet is to pay for the service or find a site that offers to compile your email lists for free.

GATHERING EMAIL LEADS

Part of creating an effective email campaign is through reaching out to the right people. Otherwise, your email is sent out into cyberspace or looked at by someone who might say, "Oh, that's nice," but has no power to further you career or help you find that dream job you are searching for. Worst of all, it can easily be construed or thought of as SPAM, which can either get you blacklisted from a potential employer or at the least annoy him or her enough to not want anything to do with you. Opt-in emails are the best to collect, so make sure you set up something on your website or e-Resume that asks a person if he or she wants to receive your newsletter. Or, if you're swapping business cards or chatting in a newsgroup, simply ask those people if they'd like to receive your newsletter, then add them to your list.

WHAT ARE YOU GOING TO SAY IN YOUR NEWSLETTER?

You are the resource and the expert. Make sure your content establishes you as that. Here is a suggested outline of a newsletter format, based on accounting:

- Lead Article - New Tax Laws and How They Affect You (400-500 words). Insert your name and company into the article where appropriate.

- Blurb - It's Tax Time: How to Maximize Those Deductions (200-300 words). Insert your name and company into the blurb where appropriate.

- Personal Message – Mention what you're working on and your personal thoughts and tips for tax time (100-200 words). Let the tone be informal yet professional, positioning yourself as an expert in the field.

- Your Photo – Preferably something from a social or charity event, but make sure it's professional.

A newsletter is an excellent way to create a presence in your industry. A newsletter:

- Helps promote you as an expert in your field.

- Gives you the opportunity to send an informative message that allows room for you to include a link back to your website, social networking sites or professional resume.

- Offers a legitimate reason for you to maintain contact with other professionals in your field.

- Helps you to gather email addresses so long as recipients opt-in.

The following is a screenshot of a newsletter put out by a dental company. Above all, it is inviting at first glance. Then as the reader digs in, he'll find a supply of helpful information regarding dental hygiene.

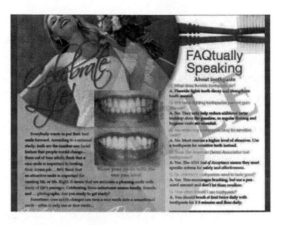

PURCHASING OR RENTING EMAIL ADDRESSES

There are several companies out there that are willing to sell or rent email lists. Here are some of the things to think about with buying vs. renting, if this is the route you choose to take. (Keep in mind that the best, most qualified emails are from people you have personally been in contact with or who have signed up proactively for your newsletter. Bigger is not always better. A smaller, more qualified email list may produce better results versus mass emailing to a huge list of unknowns.)

Buying

- Pro: You have the control of your lists, can add them to your current database and physically see the email addresses you are sending them to.

- Con: They can cost quite a bit. Plus, it's critical you research the company you are purchasing from to avoid getting a dead or spam list.

Renting

- Pro: Less expensive than purchasing.

- Con: Less security. You are supplied a list of emails but you are not allowed to see who you are sending your messages to. This can be tricky, as it involves extra research into the credibility of the company you are renting your list from and offers the risk of you double-messaging someone already on your personal list. Double-messaging will make you look like a spammer rather than a professional in the industry. Still, if your funds are limited and this is your only access to a list of professionals in your industry, it may be a risk worth taking.

VOLUNTEER

There is no better or more worthwhile way to get your name out in the community than through volunteering your time to worthy causes. Not only does it give you the opportunity to help humanity, you also get to help yourself and your career by creating the contacts you need to get ahead. But be true to yourself. Don't volunteer for something simply because you think it might help get you a job. Volunteer for those things that are important to you. If you are genuinely interested in something, this will show through naturally to employers and recruiters.

For example, Louise received recognition through her talent agency for her contributions to the "Take a Stand Against Domestic Violence" campaign. Not only does this help her gain recognition in her industry, it helps promote her as more than just a model.

AUSTIN MODELS & TALENT'S LOUISE IS SPOKESPERSON/MODEL FOR DEPARTMENT OF DEFENSE BACKED PROGRAM, "TAKE A STAND AGAINST DOMESTIC VIOLENCE."

The Austin Models & Talent Agency is proud to have Kelli (Louise) as the key spokesperson in an advertising campaign for the "Take a Stand Against Domestic Violence," which is backed by the United States Department of Defense.

How to Make Volunteering Work for You

- Choose charities sponsored by the companies you are interested in working for. That way, you know your time is spent with a cause that the company believes in, upping your odds of meeting the right people at the event or getting noticed on a resume due to your work with their charity of choice.

- Join the Board. Wherever possible, do what it takes to become a board member for those events that are heavily sponsored by your company of choice. Being on the board substantially increases your odds of working directly with the heavy hitters and also gives you the power to assign yourself to work the events you know they will attend.

- Do outstanding work! The last thing you want to do is volunteer your time to an organization and get a reputation for being late, not following through or generally coasting. You need to treat your volunteer work with the same passion and dedication you would bring to your dream job, which is why you should really be personally passionate about the organization you're volunteering for.

- Showcase your affiliations. Be certain to add your volunteering work to your resume, especially linking your resume online to the organization you are volunteering for.

CREATIVE TECHNIQUE

Be Newsworthy

Most people like to see their name in print, and when you're the one being quoted by the local newspaper about the latest trends in the industry, nothing could be better. In addition to being an expert, you can also create your own newsworthy events, within your field of expertise, which would make the media take notice.

What if you convinced your boss to let you host a "Free tax returns for 24-hrs" promotion? You could publicize the event and take on the responsibility of accurately completing as many free tax returns as possible within a 24-hour period. Not only does this create exposure for your current company (which your boss will like), it shows you as a thinker and a doer (which your potential employer will like). In addition, you are the boss of the campaign. That means you can promote it however you like to whomever you like. Include it in your social networking profiles, on your website, in newsgroups, and online communities.

Once your promotion is established and the details are finalized, announce it to the press through a press release. (And don't forget to post the press release in all of your outlets online as well.) Call your radio station to see if they'll do a live remote during the event. Invite a reporter to submit his taxes as one of the ones you'll complete.

Promotions grab the attention of those in your industry, giving you a reputation as a visionary or, at the very least, someone hungry enough to make the effort.

Provide a Useful and Branded Item

Everyone loves something for free. Pens, mouse pads, key chains, coffee mugs – anything that's useful that can include your name and website. The power of promotional items is a marketing tool that has been around for years. And since we're basically talking about marketing you, *you* should have your own promotional items, too.

Full-Color Fabric Mouse Pad
Item #14746

This is the perfect medium for displaying your promotional logo and message. Printed in full color, these mousepads display your advertising dramatically and effectively.

* Also available in sizes: 6" x 8", 7 1/2" x 8", 8" round, or with medium-duty, latex-free rubber base; call for quotes
* Heavy-duty foam rubber base

JUST ASK

One of the best ways to get in front of the right people is to ASK. Call the HR director of hiring officer of your dream company and simply ask for a meeting. Even if they say they aren't hiring, if you can persuade them to simply let you come in for five minutes to "drop off your resume," you have made an impression. While this means you have to make a cold call, a cold call is sometimes better than no call at all.

TIPS TO MAKING A STRONG COLD CALL

Do Your Research Before Picking Up the Phone

- Who are you calling? What do you know about them? What do you know about the company? All of this research must be done prior to picking up the phone. You need to wow the person on the other end of the line and convince him or her that you're worth meeting with – it's in their best interest.

Do Not Ask Questions

- Asking questions like, "Can I have a minute of your time?" gives your prospect an out. Never ask a question until you have clearly stated your business and what it is you want.

Use a Script

- Write a script to follow when calling. It may read something like:

  "Hello, this is Dan Smith calling from Peer Accounting. I saw that you recently opened and immediately closed the position for Senior Accountant. So that I don't miss out on future opportunities with your company, I would like to come in for a face-to-face meeting to get on file with your HR department. When would be a good time for you?"

- Often, you will be reading this script to a receptionist who will cut you off and connect you to the correct department. Best to allow this to happen instead of just asking to speak with someone in HR. Otherwise, you are starting your conversation with a question, giving the person on the other end the control.

Be ready to pitch.

- If opportunity knocks, you must be on your game. If you have the opportunity to talk about who you are and what you do, it should be as concise and prepared as the script above.

Gather Information

- Always probe for more information but without being a nuisance. This can be achieved through politeness and persistence. Always thank people for their time and ask productive follow-up questions such as:

  » If you do not do face-to-face pre-screening, could you recommend the best way to get my foot in the door at your company?

  » Whose attention should I make my further correspondence to?

  » When would be a good time to speak with the office manager or HR manager?

Make a Commitment to Follow Through

It doesn't matter who this commitment is made to, it gives you the honest opportunity to call back later and say, "This is Dan Smith calling from Peer Accounting. I told _____ I would follow up with you today. I saw that you recently opened and immediately closed the position for Senior Accountant. So that I don't miss out on future opportunities with your company, I would like to come in for a face-to-face meeting to get on file with your HR department. When would be a good time for you?"

Although it may seem redundant, companies receive hundreds, if not thousands, of phone calls per day. Politeness and persistence will eventually get you noticed.

Market Yourself to the Mole

Whether you are on the CareerMole or not, using all of your resources to get to someone who currently works at your dream company is an ideal way to make contact.

Email Format

Sometimes email is the best way to "cold call," since it is a non-intrusive way of approaching someone regarding a position within the company. It allows the recipient to answer on his or her terms, but yet still portrays you as professional who is a bit sensitive to the recipient's time. If the contact is responsive, ask when a good time might be to call to chat further.

WEB 2.0 ASSESSMENT #8

Your last assignment – putting it all together. It's time to create your action plan. Write down on paper – yes, actually write it down – your ultimate dream job. Describe it in detail and picture it in your mind to the point where you can see yourself in that position. Now choose three job search engines, three social networking sites, and one place to post your resume in addition to the website you'll create for your brand. Start a blog, join a newsgroup and build a list of those people and/or companies you want to network with. Now create a timeline for when each of these items will unfold in your branding campaign. Stay on track. Stay focused. Measure what works and what doesn't and refine tasks as you need to. Make sure everything you do ties back to landing that dream job. And someday it won't be a dream anymore – it will be reality.

PARTING WORDS...

The power of marketing is in your hands. Web 2.0 has given all of us the format and platform to make a name for ourselves not only in our career, but in our world. Take advantage of all the marketing opportunities you have at your disposal to maximize your presence in your professional field. The more your "brand" is seen and heard, the more likely you are to have someone remember it.

Now that you have the tools and resources to land your dream job, pursue it with all of your might. Your job search should be conducted with the same diligence and effort as a full-time job. In other words, you should devote at least eight hours of the day to making your dreams a reality. Get out there and make finding your dream job your full-time job today!

"LUCK IS WHAT HAPPENS WHEN PREPARATION MEETS OPPORTUNITY."

- LUCIUS ANNAEUS SENECA

ABOUT THE AUTHOR

Todd Bavol, PHR, is the President/CEO of the Integrity Group of companies. He is a CEO Hall of Fame member and has led his company to rank #2 on the INC 500 fastest growing privately held companies in the U.S. Todd has helped thousands of people find new careers and is passionate about teaching people skills that give them an edge in a competitive job market. Todd is an active social networker known as the JobSearchNinja on Twitter – follow him there. Todd lives in Hockessin, DE.